D1215300

amazing ships

CONTAINER SHIPS AND OIL TANKERS

JONATHAN SUTHERLAND AND DIANE CANWELL

Gareth Stevens
Publishing

CENTRAL ARKANSAS LIBRARY SYSTEM
OLEY ROOKER BRANCH
LITTLE ROCK, ARKANSAS

Please visit our web site at: www.garethstevens.com
For a free color catalog describing Gareth Stevens Publishing's list of
high-quality books, call 1-800-542-2595 (USA) or 1-800-387-3178 (Canada).

Library of Congress Cataloging-in-Publication Data available on request.

ISBN: 978-0-8368-8377-0 (lib. bdg.)

This North American edition first published in 2008 by
Gareth Stevens Publishing
A Weekly Reader® Company
1 Reader's Digest Road
Pleasantville, NY 10570-7000 USA

Copyright © 2008 Amber Books Ltd

Produced by Amber Books Ltd., Bradley's Close,
74–77 White Lion Street, London N1 9PF, U.K.

Project Editor: James Bennett
Copy Editors: Natasha Reed, Chris McNab
Design: Colin Hawes

Gareth Stevens managing editor: Mark Sachner
Gareth Stevens editor: Alan Wachtel
Gareth Stevens art direction: Tammy West
Gareth Stevens production: Jessica Yanke

All illustrations courtesy of Art-Tech/Aerospace

Photo credits:
5: New Orleans Steam Boat Company, 7: Cody Images, 9: Canadian Coast Guard, 11: Getty Images (Stringer), 13: Dockwise Shipping B.V., 15: Bergensen Gas Worldwide, 16: Shell, 19: Chevron, 21: Global Marine Systems Limited, 23: Jan de Nul Group, 25: Maersk Line, 27: Getty Images (Peter Essick), 29: Flying Focus

All rights reserved. No part of this book may be reproduced,
stored in a retrieval system, or transmitted in any form or
by any means, electronic, mechanical, photocopying, recording,
or otherwise, without the prior written permission of the
copyright holder.

Printed in the United States of America

1 2 3 4 5 6 7 8 9 11 10 09 08 07

NATCHEZ

Natchez was a side-wheel **steamship** built to transport cotton, mail, and passengers up and down the Mississippi River. She was launched in Cincinnati in 1869. She sailed the Mississippi River for 9 1/2 years, making 401 trips between New Orleans and the town of Natchez. In June 1870, she achieved fame when she beat her rival, the *Robert E. Lee,* in a race between New Orleans and St. Louis.

KEY FACTS

• Nine side-wheel steamships have been named *Natchez.* The ship illustrated below was actually the sixth to be given the name.

• The ninth *Natchez,* launched in 1975, can still be seen on the Mississippi River at New Orleans. It is now a floating restaurant and pleasure boat.

The ship's main paddle wheel was powered by a huge piston from the engine room.

The *Natchez's* main cargo was bales of cotton.

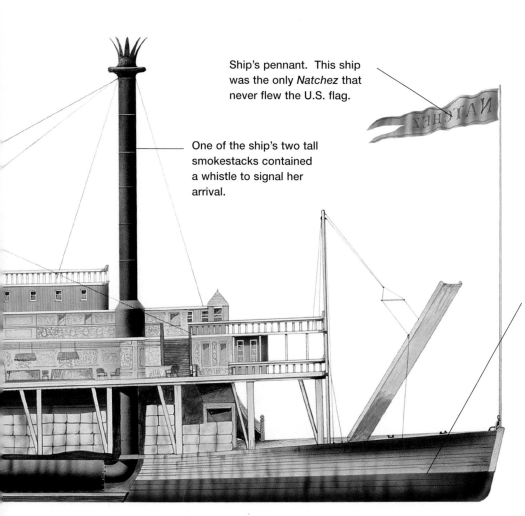

Ship's pennant. This ship was the only *Natchez* that never flew the U.S. flag.

One of the ship's two tall smokestacks contained a whistle to signal her arrival.

The modern *Natchez* has a paddle wheel at the rear instead of the side-wheel used on many of the older boats.

The ship's **hull** had a **draft** of only 10 feet (3 meters).

Did You Know?

The name *Natchez* originally came from the Natchez Native American tribe that lived along the lower Mississippi River.

PREUSSEN

The *Preussen* was a five-masted sailing ship built in Hamburg, Germany, in 1902. In November 1910, she collided with a British steamship, the SS *Brighton*, in the English Channel in fog. The *Preussen* was heavily damaged and abandoned at sea while still afloat. She was eventually wrecked on the English coast at Dover.

Did You Know?

The *Preussen's* sail area was a massive 59,848 square feet (5,559 sq m). She was the only five-masted full-**rigged** ship ever built. "Full-rigged" means that all her main sails were carried on horizontal **spars**.

KEY FACTS

- In her time, the *Preussen* was the largest sailing ship ever built without back-up engines.
- She was 480 feet (146 m) long.

The *Preussen* had a total of 48 sails.

Steel hull

Cargo holds for up to 800 tons (726 metric tons) of goods

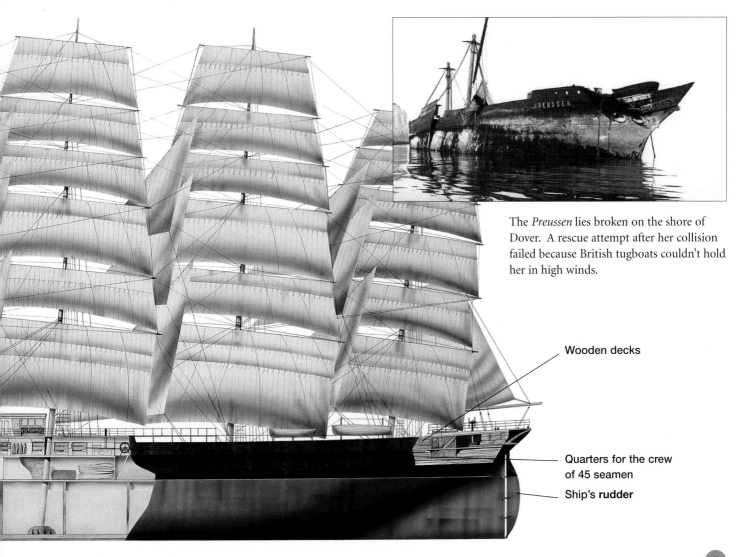

The *Preussen* lies broken on the shore of Dover. A rescue attempt after her collision failed because British tugboats couldn't hold her in high winds.

Wooden decks

Quarters for the crew of 45 seamen

Ship's **rudder**

CCGS Louis St. Laurent

This Canadian coastguard **icebreaker** was named after the twelfth prime minister of Canada. The *Louis St. Laurent* was built in 1969 in Montreal and later underwent a major upgrade in Halifax, Nova Scotia, between 1988 and 1993. She has been based at Dartmouth, Nova Scotia, for her entire career. In the summer, she voyages to Canada's arctic region.

Did You Know?

During her upgrade, she was given new engines and new navigation systems, and her hull was lengthened. The whole process took five years.

KEY FACTS

• The *St. Laurent* brings supplies to coastal communities in the Arctic, breaks ship lanes through icy waters, and also transports scientific expeditions.

• She is the largest icebreaker in the Canadian Coastguard Fleet.

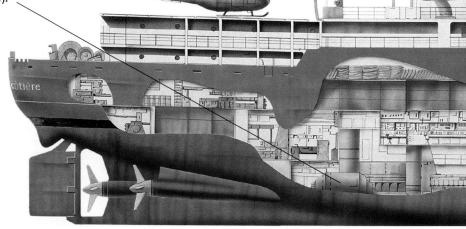

Communications antenna. The ship is fitted with many different types of radio and navigation systems.

Diesel-electric motors. These engines give the ship a top speed of 20 **knots** (37 kilometers per hour).

One of a pair of BO-105 helicopters

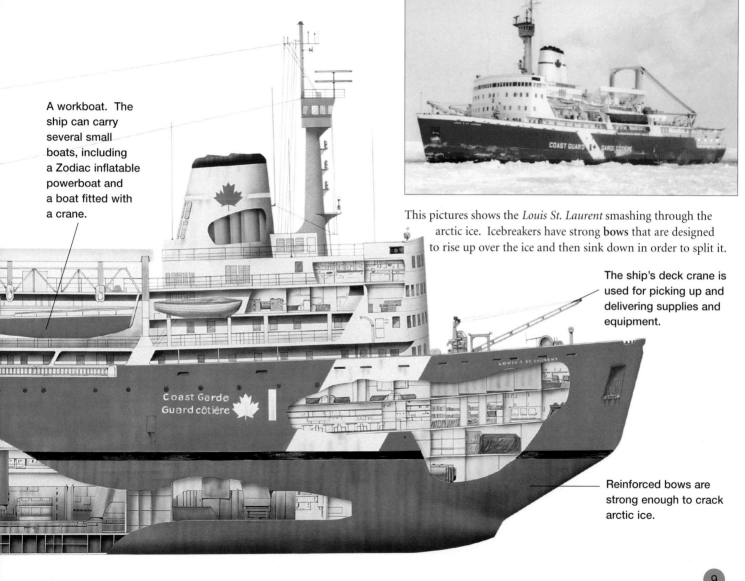

A workboat. The ship can carry several small boats, including a Zodiac inflatable powerboat and a boat fitted with a crane.

This pictures shows the *Louis St. Laurent* smashing through the arctic ice. Icebreakers have strong **bows** that are designed to rise up over the ice and then sink down in order to split it.

The ship's deck crane is used for picking up and delivering supplies and equipment.

Reinforced bows are strong enough to crack arctic ice.

GALILEO

The *Galileo* is a British vessel designed to carry liquid petroleum gas (LPG). Built in 1982, she can carry more than 2,000,000 cubic feet (60,000 cubic meters) of gas. She sails between ports in Australia, the Persian Gulf, and Europe.

Did You Know?
In 1997, two of the *Galileo*'s crew were shot and wounded during a raid by pirates at the Petrobras Oil Terminal, in Brazil.

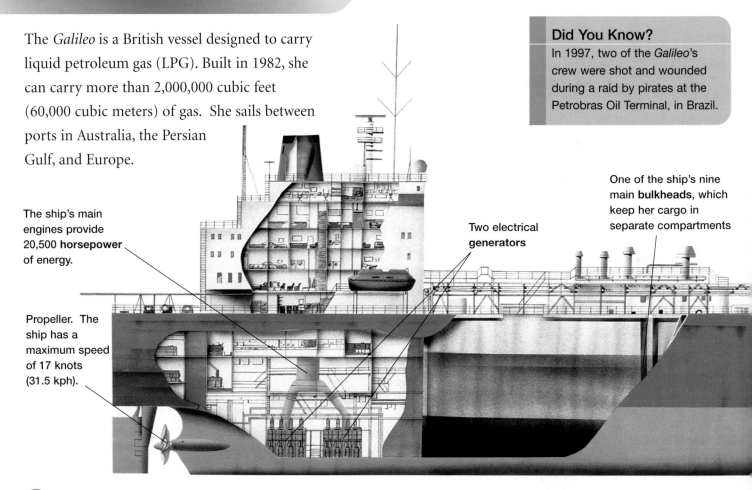

The ship's main engines provide 20,500 **horsepower** of energy.

Propeller. The ship has a maximum speed of 17 knots (31.5 kph).

Two electrical **generators**

One of the ship's nine main **bulkheads**, which keep her cargo in separate compartments

KEY FACTS

• When it is fully loaded, the *Galileo* carries up to $20 million worth of gas.

• LPG provides about 3 percent of all the energy consumed in the United States.

Ships including the *Galileo* and the famous *Titanic* were built by Harland and Wolff, a company based in Northern Ireland. The company was formed in 1861.

The Galileo's hull is 984 feet (300 m) long.

A cargo tank. The Galileo has five cargo tanks. Each of these tanks is designed to safely hold liquid gases.

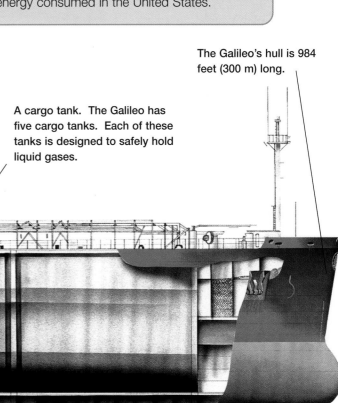

LPG

MIGHTY SERVANT 3

Built in 1984, the *Mighty Servant 3* was a semi-**submersible** vessel capable of lifting huge loads. She was designed to work in harsh weather and in deep water, lifting gas platforms, oil rigs, and even other vessels. In December 2006, she sank off the coast of Angola, in Africa. She has now been salvaged.

The ship had 131 feet x 459 feet (40 x 140 m) of deck space. The deck can hold up to 25 tons per 10 square feet (1 sq m).

Did You Know?
The ship fills internal tanks with water to lower her deck below the water's surface so cargo can be floated onto the ship.

The *Mighty Servant 3* is pictured here carrying a huge steel structure that is part of a drilling platform.

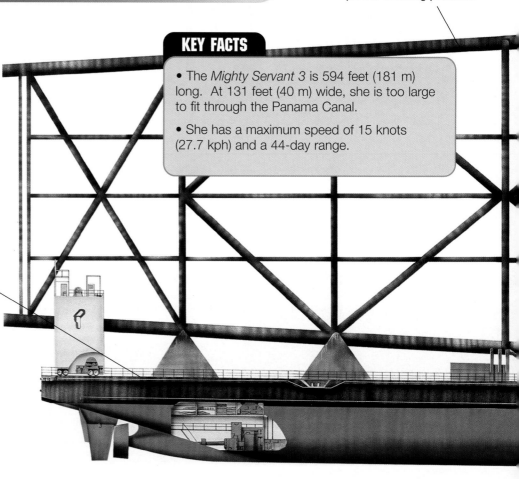

KEY FACTS

• The *Mighty Servant 3* is 594 feet (181 m) long. At 131 feet (40 m) wide, she is too large to fit through the Panama Canal.

• She has a maximum speed of 15 knots (27.7 kph) and a 44-day range.

In this picture, her sister ship, the *Mighty Servant 1*, carries on her deck a full gas platform that weighs thousands of tons.

Forward pilothouse

Pumping engines. Once the cargo is aboard, these engines pump water out of the ship's internal tanks to raise the level of her lower deck above water.

The ship has internal tanks that are flooded so her lower deck can sink below the water.

BERGE STAHL

The *Berge Stahl* is the largest bulk-cargo-carrying ship in the world. She was built in 1986 and is used by a Norwegian shipping company to carry iron ore. She picks up iron ore from the Terminal Maritimo de Ponta da Madeira, in Brazil, or the Saldanha port, in South Africa, and deposits it at the Port of Rotterdam, in the Netherlands.

Did You Know?

Because of her enormous size, the only ports that can handle the *Berge Stahl* are the ports that she visits in Brazil, South Africa, and the Netherlands.

The engine drives a single propeller.

Hyundai B+W 7L9OMCE diesel engine. This engine is 30 feet (9.1 m) tall and generates 27,610 horsepower.

30-foot- (9 meter-) tall rudder

KEY FACTS

- The *Berge Stahl* was made in South Korea by Hyundai Heavy Industries, the world's largest shipbuilder.

- The name *Berge Stahl* means "steel mountain" in Norwegian.

In this picture, the *Berge Stahl* is anchored in Ponta da Madeira, Brazil. Iron ore is being poured into her open cargo holds.

The total length of the ship's hull is 1,221 feet (372 m).

The *Berge Stahl*'s cargo holds are designed to carry iron ore.

SEAWELL

The *Seawell* was built in 1987 in Sunderland, England. She is a diving support vessel (DSV). Her purpose is to support diving operations around oil rigs and gas platforms far out at sea. She also conducts repairs on oil rigs and gas platforms, using her powerful cranes and other equipment.

The *Seawell* carried out important work on the Gannet Oilfield in the North Sea in 1997. Up to 18 divers at a time are lowered over the side of the *Seawell* in a pressurized diving bell. They live in the diving bell for days or weeks while maintaining oil rigs.

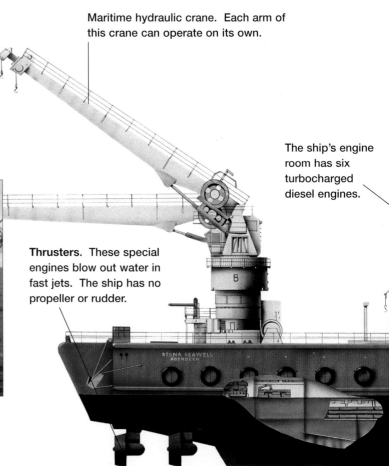

Maritime hydraulic crane. Each arm of this crane can operate on its own.

The ship's engine room has six turbocharged diesel engines.

Thrusters. These special engines blow out water in fast jets. The ship has no propeller or rudder.

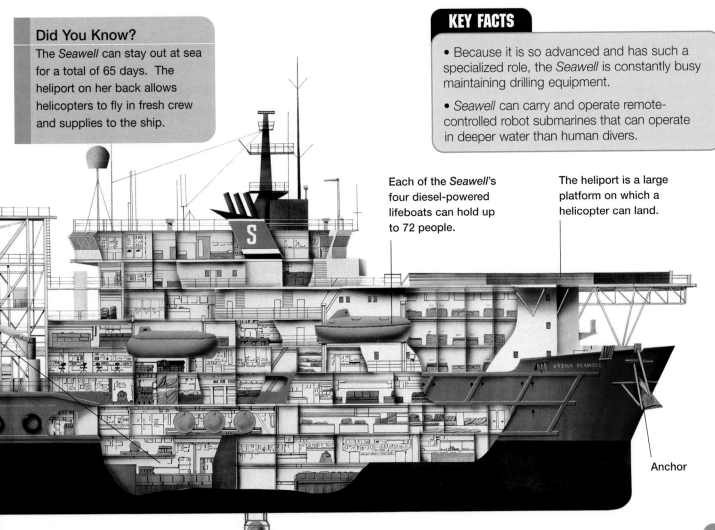

Did You Know?

The *Seawell* can stay out at sea for a total of 65 days. The heliport on her back allows helicopters to fly in fresh crew and supplies to the ship.

KEY FACTS

• Because it is so advanced and has such a specialized role, the *Seawell* is constantly busy maintaining drilling equipment.

• *Seawell* can carry and operate remote-controlled robot submarines that can operate in deeper water than human divers.

Each of the *Seawell*'s four diesel-powered lifeboats can hold up to 72 people.

The heliport is a large platform on which a helicopter can land.

STENA SEAWELL

Anchor

NORTHWEST SANDERLING

The *Northwest Sanderling* was the first vessel to carry liquefied natural gas (LNG) from northwest Australia to Japan. Mitsubushi Heavy Industries, a Japanese company, built her in its Nagasaki shipyard in 1989. She has been in use ever since, carrying millions of tons of LNG across the Pacific Ocean every year.

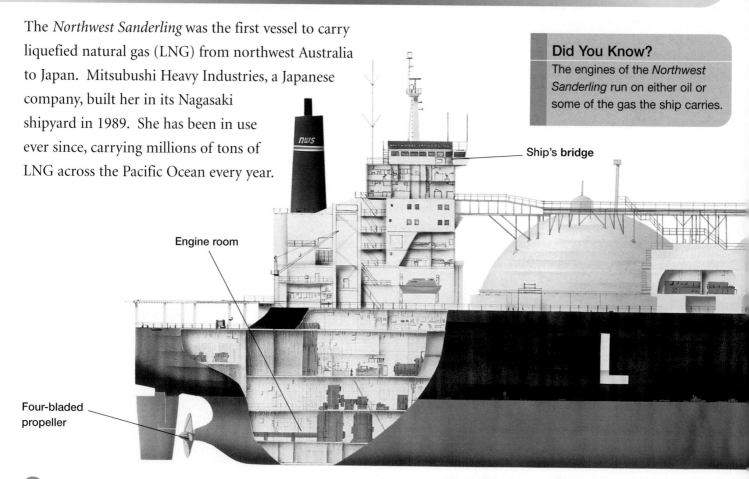

Did You Know?
The engines of the *Northwest Sanderling* run on either oil or some of the gas the ship carries.

Ship's **bridge**

Engine room

Four-bladed propeller

KEY FACTS

• The *Northwest Sanderling* can carry more than 4,400,000 cubic feet (124,900 cu m) of LNG.

• The LNG can be loaded at about 353,100 cubic feet (9,993 cu m) per hour and unloaded slightly faster.

This picture shows the *Northwest Swan*, one of the newest types of gas tanker. The gas is stored below deck, rather than in round tanks, in huge holds surrounded by nitrogen gas.

Each round gas tank is 131 feet (40 m) in diameter. The gas inside is kept very cold — about -261 °F (-163 °C).

Even though the ship is huge, the hull has a draft of just 36 feet (11 m).

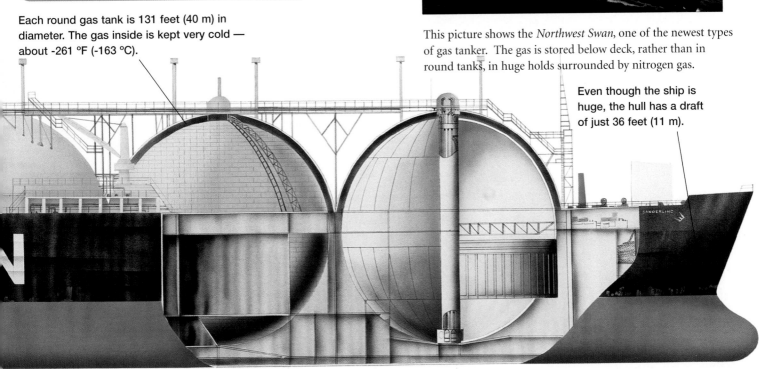

CS SOVEREIGN

The CS *Sovereign* was built in 1991 in the Netherlands. She is a vessel for laying or repairing cables on the ocean floor. Fully loaded, she can carry up to 1,700 tons (1,550 metric tons) of cable. She mainly works in the Atlantic Ocean laying communication cables. Her home port is Portland, Dorset, in England.

A crew cabin. The ship has 14 officer's cabins, 20 double crew cabins, and 22 single crew cabins.

The ship's bridge has excellent visibility all around.

Her pair of Stork Wartsila engines produce a maximum of 13,862 horsepower.

Did You Know?

The CS *Sovereign* can carry a range of remote-controlled vehicles, each about the same size as an SUV. These vehicles are used to dig trenches and bury cables in the seabed.

The *Sovereign* can carry 6,832 tons (6,200 metric tons) of cable and other equipment.

The open deck allows the ship to use many underwater vehicles, which are lowered from the deck into the water.

The CS *Sovereign* is shown here during a cable-laying operation. She was designed to cope with severe weather in the Atlantic Ocean and other rough seas.

C S SOVEREIGN

KEY FACTS

- Cable-laying is a long job, and the *Sovereign* can spend 44 days at sea.

- Her service speed is 12 knots (22 kph).

- She is 427 feet (130 m) long.

JAMES COOK

The *James Cook* is a **dredger**, a ship that scoops out earth from the bottoms of harbors or rivers. She was built in 1992 at a shipyard in Hardinxveld-Giessendam, Belgium. The vessel has operated in Dubai, Hong Kong, Malaysia, the Philippines, and Singapore.

KEY FACTS

• The *James Cook* was the largest vessel of its type when it was launched in 1992.

• The ship's normal dredging depth is 148 feet (45 m), but with special equipment it can reach down to a depth of 246 feet (75 m).

Did You Know?

The *James Cook* has had three names: the *JFJ de Nul* (1992), the *Inai Seroja* (2003), and the *James Cook* (2004).

Heavy-duty crane

Her two 8,314-horsepower engines give her a top speed of 15 knots (28 kph).

Her dredging suction pipe works like a huge vacuum cleaner.

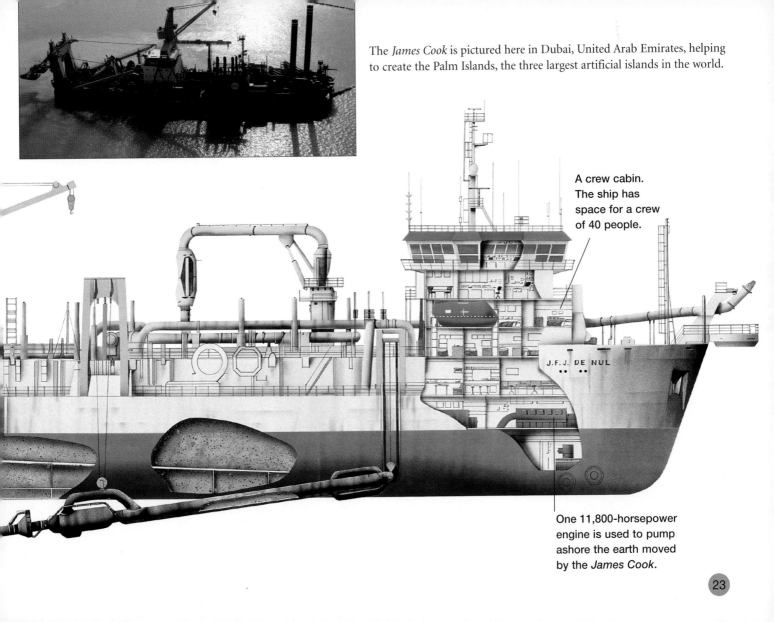

The *James Cook* is pictured here in Dubai, United Arab Emirates, helping to create the Palm Islands, the three largest artificial islands in the world.

A crew cabin. The ship has space for a crew of 40 people.

J.F.J. DE NUL

One 11,800-horsepower engine is used to pump ashore the earth moved by the *James Cook*.

JERVIS BAY

The *Jervis Bay* is a British container ship. She was built in 1992 by Ishikawajima-Harima Heavy Industries in Japan, and she can carry a huge amount of cargo, including a total of 2,850 containers. Fully loaded the ship weighs up to about 60,000 tons (54,400 metric tons).

Did You Know?

The first ship with the name *Jervis Bay* was a Royal Navy warship. The *Jervis Bay* shown here is the third container ship to bear the name.

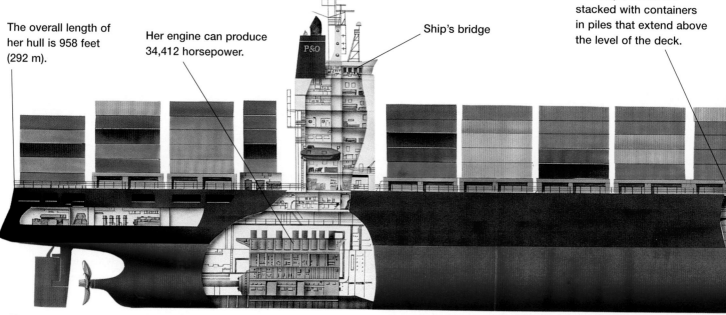

The overall length of her hull is 958 feet (292 m).

Her engine can produce 34,412 horsepower.

Ship's bridge

The ship's holds are stacked with containers in piles that extend above the level of the deck.

KEY FACTS

• The *Jervis Bay* makes eight-week round-trip voyages. It calls at ports in Singapore, Hong Kong, China, and Korea before heading back to Europe.

• She now also makes transatlantic journeys between Europe and the United States. These voyages take about two weeks.

Each container can weigh up to about 26 tons (24 metric tons).

In this picture, the *Jervis Bay* is shown fully laden with cargo. Although her containers can be stacked five or six deep, the ship's captain can still see clearly from the bridge.

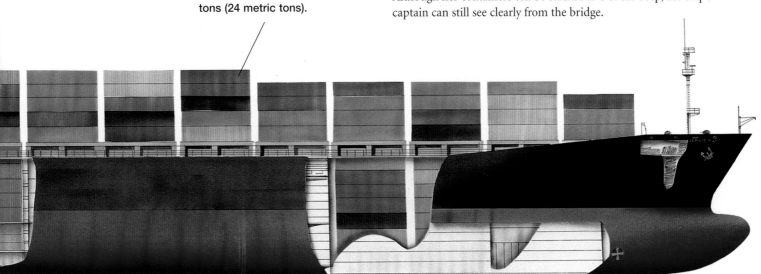

St. Lucia

The *St. Lucia* is a container ship that was built for the Geest Company in 1993. She was designed to carry bananas from the West Indies to ports all over the world. When she was launched, the *St. Lucia* could carry 40 percent more fruit than rival ships.

KEY FACTS

- The *St. Lucia* is known as a "refer" vessel because of the refrigerated containers it carries.

- *St. Lucia* weighs about 13,070 tons (11,860 metric tons).

- She has a total length of 518 feet (158 m).

Containers can be stacked up on her deck. She can carry 108 refrigerated containers.

Ship's bridge, with cabins below. The ship has a crew of 19 people.

Her single propeller is powered by a massive Hyundai engine.

Did You Know?

The *St. Lucia* carries fruit and freight among Ecuador, the United States, Japan, and New Zealand. During the kiwi fruit season, she also sails between New Zealand and Great Britain.

Bananas are lifted off a container ship. The *St. Lucia* played an important role in shipping more bananas out of the West Indies.

The St. Lucia has five levels of container storage below deck.

E

GEEST ST LUCIA

CORNELIS VROLIJK

The *Cornelis Vrolijk* is a fishing ship from the Netherlands. She is a **trawler**, or a ship that tows a net behind her to catch thousands of fish that swim near the surface of the open sea. Much of her year is spent fishing off the West African coast. The *Cornelis Vrolijk* normally operates with a crew of 37 people.

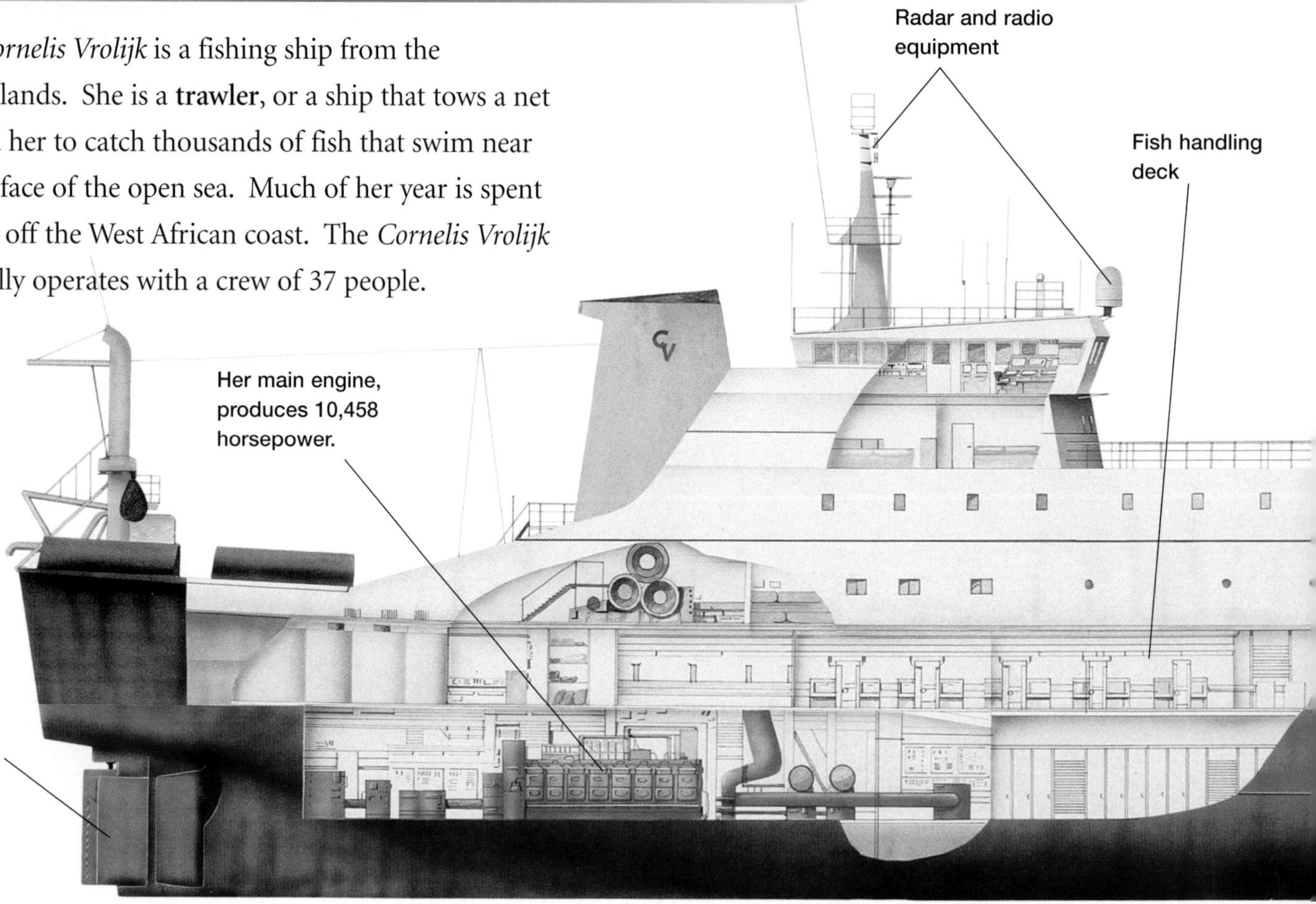

Radar and radio equipment

Fish handling deck

Her main engine, produces 10,458 horsepower.

Rudder

KEY FACTS

• Her holds can each carry 540 tons of fish.

• She is 413 feet (126 m) long.

• In tropical conditions, freezing and cooling the fish uses up to 80 percent of the ship's power.

The *Cornelis Vrolijk* tows a a type of net known as a pelagic trawl net. This net has an opening as large as five soccer fields.

Did You Know?
One of her fishing winches can pull in the fishing net at a speed of 236 feet (72 m) per second, and another pulls in the net at 249 feet (76 m) per second.

Freezers. The fish she catches are frozen by 40 frosting machines.

SCH 171

GLOSSARY

bow the front part of a ship

bridge the part of a ship where the navigation and steering equipment is usually found and from where the ship is controlled

bulkhead a vertical wall that divides up a ship into separate compartments

cargo hold a space in which cargo is stored

draft the depth that the lowest part of the ship reaches beneath the surface of the water

dredger a ship that is designed to remove material from a seabed or riverbed

generator a machine that is used to create electricity to run motors, lights, and tools

horsepower a unit of measure for the power of an engine

hull the main body of a ship, the part that allows it to float

icebreaker a ship designed to cut through waters that are covered with ice

knot a unit for measuring the speed of ships, which is equivalent to 1.15 miles per hour (1.8 kph)

pilothouse a small room on the bridge of a ship that contains all the instruments for steering ("piloting") a ship

rigged having a system of ropes, wires, and chains used to control the sails of a ship

rudder a hinged device fitted at the rear of a ship and used to steer the craft

spars thick wood or metal pieces used to support rigging

steamship any ship that uses steam engines for its main source of power

submersible a vessel that can go underwater; "semi-submersible" means it can go partly underwater

thruster an engine used to keep a ship steady in one place or to push it slowly into position

trawler a type of fishing vessel that catches fish using a large net

FOR MORE INFORMATION

BOOKS

- *All About Ships.* All About (series). Chris Oxlade (Southwater)

- *The Golden Age of Shipping: The Classic Merchant Ship 1900—1960.* Conway's History of the Ship (series). Robert Gardiner and Ambrose Greenway (Chartwell)

- *The Great Ships.* Patrick O'Brien. (Walker Books)

- *The World of Ships.* The World of (series). Philip Wilkinson (Kingfisher)

WEB SITES

- Canadian Coastguard Service
  www.ccg-gcc.gc.ca

- Dockwise Fleet: Open Deck Vessels
  www.dockwise.com/?sid=10

- Global Marine Systems: the CS Sovereign
  www.globalmarinesystems.com/ships/ships_cs_sovereign.asp

Publishers note to educators and parents:

Our editors have carefully reviewed these Web sites to ensure that they are suitable for children. Many web sites change frequently, however, and we cannot guarantee that a site's future contents will continue to meet our high standards of quality and educational value. Be advised that children should be closely supervised whenever they access the internet.

INDEX